QEⅡ
WE ♥ YOU

QE II
WE ♥ YOU

A child's-eye celebration of Queen Elizabeth II

First published in Great Britain in 2015 by
Michael O'Mara Books Limited
9 Lion Yard
Tremadoc Road
London SW4 7NQ

A CIP catalogue record for this book is available from the British Library.

Papers used by Michael O'Mara Books Limited are natural, recyclable
products made from wood grown in sustainable forests. The manufacturing
processes conform to the environmental regulations of the country of origin.

ISBN: 978-1-78243-416-0 in hardback print format

1 2 3 4 5 6 7 8 9 10

Printed and bound in Malaysia

www.mombooks.com

CONTENTS

BEING THE QUEEN

RELAXATION

THE QUEEN AND I

INTRODUCTION

Children often view the greatest of ideas, traditions and institutions with a refreshing simplicity adults lack, and there is little that is more complex and enduring than the British monarchy.

To mark Queen Elizabeth II becoming the longest-reigning British monarch, children from a number of primary schools were asked for their thoughts on the queen, her work and her life. Their answers and drawings offer charming, amusing and sometimes surprising insights into both the queen's life and the minds of children.

Divided into sections on the queen's life and work, how she relaxes and children's relationship with the queen, the responses featured illustrate the truly unique way children view the world and their place in it.

croan

dog

shoos

The queen is byooeful.

The queen is luckee.

The queen has lovlee dogs.

8

AMÉLIE, age 6

BEING THE QUEEN

WHO IS THE QUEEN?

The Queen is Queen Elizabeth II and She lives in a palise.

OLIVIA, age 9

I think the Queen is a ~~woman~~ woman with fancy clothes.

TYMEK, age 9

9

The queen is someone who is in charge of the unitite kingdom.

MICHELLE, age 9

the Queen is Somebody who is in charge and mabye in charge of the entire kingdom and that is very important because if she wasen't Here the world would of been boring and She has changed the world.

KATIE, age 9

ANNA, age 8

WHAT IS THE QUEEN'S NAME?

The Queen first name is Elizabeth and her surname is Mary II.

KATY, age 9

The Queens first name is Elizabeth and her surname is the second.

STEPHANIE, age 9

HOW OLD IS THE QUEEN?

The queen *is* like 88 years old because she has been alive for 88 years.

RICO, age 9

The Queen is 99 and is 100 on 30th July 2014. She will get her letter from everyone in great britain.

HARRY, age 10

I think the queen is about 49. Years old.

MIA, age 9

This is the old queen ~~woer weitting~~ wearing ~~to~~ her ~~jewls~~ Jewlerry.

ZAINEB, age 8

HARRY, age 10

The Queen is 88 years old. She was born 21st of April 1926. The Queen is lucky because She has 2 birthdays 1 on June and 1 in april?

TAFARI, age 9

I think the Queen is loo yeas old because she is wrinkly, grey hair, walks Slowly. She Might need a stick I do not know.

MOLLY, age 10

15

16

CERI, age 8

WHERE DOES THE QUEEN LIVE?

I think the Queen lives in london in Buckingham palace because I have seen her come out of the door.

GEMMA, age 10

The queen lives in brixton or probely in Kings avenue.

MIA, age 9

~~The~~ ~~queen~~ ~~lives~~ ~~in~~
~~pucking~~ ~~and~~ ~~palace~~.

JOEY, age 9

17

The Qween lives in a very big Palace in buckingham.

TASHANA, age 9

In Bukanim palice.

BORODEJ, age 8

The queen lives in crystil place.

METI, age 8

18

ALEX, age 7

The Queen lives in Buckinham Palace which is in England but it might be a little far from here.

KATIE, age 9

This is the Queen outside her house.

MARJANA, age 8

Buckingham
Palace

XANTHIA, age 10

WHAT DOES THE QUEEN LIKE?

qeen watching Engerand

BILLY, age 8

HOW DOES THE QUEEN GET TO WORK IN THE MORNING?

I think the Queen goes by bus to work to meet public

TYMEK, age 9

With a nice milky brew with a horse and a... Carridge !!!

ANDREA, age 10

The queen gets to work by a limo her Servants drive the limo for her?

TAFARI, age 9

23

I think she goes to work on a really old car so she doesn't get noticed by the public. The Queen is 78 years old, I think.

JOANNA, age 10

She goes in a private jet or in a limo.

DOUGLAS, age 9

I Think the Queen gets to work in a carriage

STEPHANIE, age 10

24

JESSICA, age 7

The queen is in a airplane.

WHAT DOES THE QUEEN DO ALL DAY?

She signs papers and hands out medals.

ALANNA, age 9

She reads, boss people around, Make notes and shout.

KATY, age 9

The Queen sits on her throne and reads the newspaper all day.

STEPHANIE, age 9

27

The Qween Sings Letters that come in a red box allday. She has no now choice bob to sing them even if She does not Want to.

TASHANA, age 9

I Think the Queen does yoga in the morning and work in the afternoon.

STEPHANIE, age 10

She listens to the birds sing the anthem.

LUISA, age 9

28

The queen is outside with her
dog and wearing crown and Jewles

KHADIJA, age 8

The   Queen   tels
You   Wat   To   do.

AMY, age 4

The Queen signs paper and she dosn't have a choice.

RICO, age 9

The Queen rings the waiter bell all day'.

MATTHIAS, age 9

the queen sits in the thorn and drink wine also go' to meeting :

JADA, age 9

31

She Sits on her throne and judges people.

AIDAN, age 8

She waves to the people outside and has meatings,

DOUGLAS, age 9

She think's how to make our country better.

KYM, age 8

32

The queen is whith her
~~kwow~~ Crown and her Jnwle's.

LAMISHA, age 8

The queen is walking to the crown bat the soldier thinks she's a theif

FRANKIE, age 8

HOW LONG HAS SHE BEEN QUEEN?

The Queen is 88 years old which means shes been Queen for 61 years!

CHLOE, age 9

She has bee the Queen for 61 years.

MICHELLE, age 9

35

WHAT DOES THE QUEEN WEAR?

The queen wears a red dress a crown and silver cape.

LEAH, age 9

The queen wears posh clothes for example a posh cape, a posh crown, a posh shirt, some posh trouses and posh shoes.

BORODEJ, age 8

The Queen wears a crown and lots of jwelary and lots of beautiful dresses to match with the things that she is wearing.

KATIE, age 9

36

ANNISA, age 8

the qeen wears~~t~~
a formal dress

MORGAN, age 8

The queen whears a wite wite dress with lots of sparkles on it anda shiny crown on her head.

TASHANA, age 9

The Queen wears dresses and very nice hats tha have very nice flower on them.

MICHELLE, age 9

The queen wears silky clothes, shining jewellry and beautiful Crowns and tiaras. Also lots of cream colours.

CHLOE, age 9

TEGAN, age 6

40

This is the Qeen wearing her besbest
clothes andtis with her pets and is walking
to her carigre. A Srvenant is leading a horse,
Trafigre sqaure is in the back round. So is her house.

ZOE, age 8

RELAXATION

WHAT DOES THE QUEEN WATCH ON TV?

The Queen likes to watch her citizens
gail on 'You've been gramed'!

MATTHIAS, age 9

I think the queen likes to watch Songs of
Praise, because they always sing God Save the
Queen!

YSOBELLE, age 9

I think the Queen watches
Eastenders or Coronation Street
because older people like watching
drama series.

TYMEK, age 9

her   selve
to   see   how
she   looks

RYAN, age 8

East Enders because she likes to shout at the TV whenever something bad is happening.

I think the queen watches how to be a better queen and disney XD.

44

I know What the Queen Watches Spongebob because She always is happy and So is Spongebob.

ETHAN, age 10

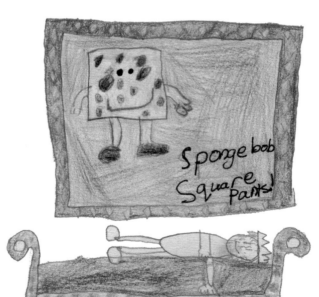

JACK, age 10

45

MEGAN, age 7

WHAT DOES THE QUEEN DO AT THE WEEKEND?

She watches films about kings and queens to see if the actors are very good

CHARLIE, age 10

I think Queen Elizabeth likes to look after her Corgis at the weekend.

I think She could teach me how to look after dogs responsibly

CATHERINE, age 9

The queen forget to go to work so She stays Right where She is.

DAN, age 9

What does the Queen do at the weekend? Has late night partys and gets told off.

ERIN, age 10

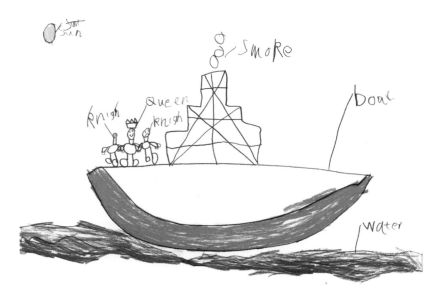

ELIASZ, age 6

48

STEPHANIE, age 10

49

WHAT HOBBIES DO YOU THINK THE QUEEN HAS?

I think the queens hobbie is Swimming because the queen was good at Swimming when she was 13.

GRACE, age 10

Being head of the UK, wearing her precious crown

AIDAN, age 8

I think the queen likes to swim and running

MIA, age 9

The queen playing a game whatching tv

KEIRA, age 8

I think she plays with her dogs and does Golf or hockey.

BRIANNA, age 8

51

reading the newspaper
barking at the dogs
waving
being ritch

RYAN, age 8

I think the Queens hobbies include waving money and playing minecraft.

JACK, age 10

BEA, age 8

WHERE DOES THE QUEEN GO ON HOLIDAY?

The Queen goes to Germany
to buy awesome gadgets.

YSOBELLE, age 9

The Queen goes to Scotaland and Antantica.
(to vist the Penguns).

MIA, age 9

I think the Queen gose to Frane because
It gall of amazing Tandmaskes.

NAOMI, age 9

RYAN, age 8

BEN, age 8

I think it's France because France is hot and sunny.

CHARLIE, age 10

56

I think she ~~(gos)~~ goes to Countries that don't have meuch water and food.

BRIANNA, age 8

DANIEL, age 8

I think the queen goes to Italy on her holidays because it is hot and very lovley and nice.

GRACE, age 10

The Queen On the beach.

OLIVIA, age 10

NEVE, age 10

WHAT DOES THE QUEEN DO ON HOLIDAY?

She goes to sun attractions.

CHARLIE, age 10

LAILA, age 8

She plays miniture goly and eats tomatoe soup.

ERIN, age 10

WHAT IS THE QUEEN'S FAVOURITE FOOD?

I think that the Queen likes to eat fancy lobster or salmon from expensive cafe's in London, but she seceretly nips into KFC for breakfast.

OLIVIA, age 10

The Queen favourite food is fish fingers and chips and jelly.

STEPHANIE, age 9

Her favourite food is tee bone staek, medium are.

HARRY, age 10

HARRY, age 8

I think Queen Elizabeth likes to eat her favourite foods at the weekends too. They might be roast turkey, pork pies, cake, vegetables and fruit.

CATHERINE, age 10

I think the Queen eats posh food because she is posh and posh food goes with posh people.

GEMMA, age 10

Mushy peas because old people like mushy peas

CHARLIE, age 10

The Queens favourite food is ribs with chips and fish and chip also spice chicken wing.

MIA, age 9

JOANNA, age 10

I think the Queens favorite food is a gull english breakfast. I also think the Queens favorite meal is breakfast because of this.

GRACE, age 9

I think the Queen's favourite food is McDonalds however she keeps it a secret because she doesn't tell anyone just incase if people laugh at her.

JOANNA, age 10

66

The queen is eating
her lunch, a plate
of cucumbers.

NAFIZ, age 8

The Queen is with her 8 pets.

woof

Dog

bunny

cat

Poodel

68

LYLA, age 8

WHAT IS THE QUEEN'S FAVOURITE ANIMAL?

I think the Queens favourite, animal
is a dog because She has Corgis

GEMMA, age 10

I believe the Queen loves dogs the best,

but She loves all animals too.

STEPHANIE, age 10

The animals the queen likes are dogs and
cats.

METI, age 8

The Queen likes snakes, dogs and hippos

MIA, age 9

The Queen likes dogs thats why she lives with two dogs.

RICO, age 9

Since she has dogs as pets I think she likes dogs. Her dogs are Corgis.

CHLOE, age 9

70

GRACIE, age 10

The Queen is playing with her corgis.

72

The Queen put her corgis on the lead because they were too excited but one og the corgis was being good but she diden't let it og the lead just yet.

EMMA, age 6

73

THE QUEEN AND I

DO YOU LIKE THE QUEEN?

I like the Queen because she is polite and helpful.

AMY, age 8

I don't like the queen because I don't vote and I'm Irish.

CALEB, age 8

I dit like the queen because what has she done for us children? Nothink absolutly nothink.

PREYA, age 9

AMELIE, age 10

75

LILLY, age 6

I do not like the queen because shes not helping england by not stopping roberry and bad stuff like that.

HALIL, age 9

Yes I Like the queen because She helps us She **control** peepl and She wrocke for us.

JESSIE, age 9

I do like the queen because She is Kinde and She is verry helpull and she dident complane that she Dosen't want to be the Queen. The queen even dident have a retiremant

OLIVIA, age 9

77

Yes I do like the Queen because
if we didn't have her then who would
come up with the brilliant ideas.

XANTHIA, age 10

Yes because she is so
old and she still working
for our country.

KYM, age 8

I don't like the queen because we have to
pay tax.

DAVINA, age 8

HENRY, age 7

I don't like the Queen because I think her job is boring and she has to read every single day.

KATY, age 9

The queen wearing her crown.

MAX, age 8

WHY DO YOU LIKE THE QUEEN?

I like the queen because she makes the
right choices.

METI, age 8

I do like the Queen because she has never
complained about what she does.

CHLOE, age 9

We love the Queen because she is
very nice and the best Queen
we have had so far.

KATIE, age 9

becauseshe brings money from tourism.

MORGAN, age 8

I like the Queen because she helped me through my life.

KYM, age 8

I like the queen because she mack amazing decisions that we all like.

JESSIE, age 9

FREDDIE, age 7

WHAT WOULD YOU SAY TO THE QUEEN IF YOU SAW HER?

I'd keep quiet, to not be charged with Treason!

ANDREA, age 10

how old are you

HARRY, age 7

Hello queen I sugest you go home now theres no need to come.

LUISA, age 9

84

The green

MILLIE, age 8

I would say "Hellow Its a Plesur to meet you on this fine day.

NAOMI, age 9

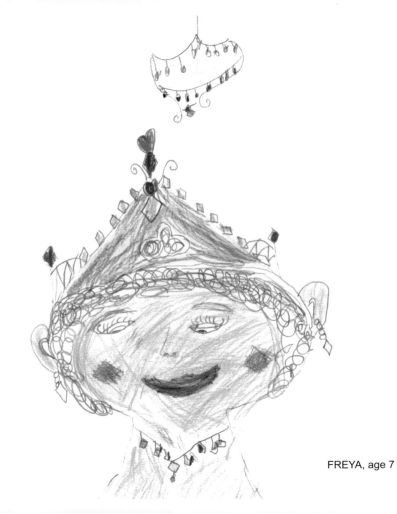

FREYA, age 7

86

how many TV's do you have.

RAPHAEL, age 8

"Hello you look very pretty to day."

DOMINIC, age 8

hellou Queen you are the best do you know that.

CHRISTOPHER, age 8

I would say "you have met my uncle" to the Queen.

RICO, age 9

I will welcome her and thank her for what she has done for us.

KYM, age 8

I would say something like Hello my Queen its a great pleasure to meet you. I would also say I have many questions for you.

CHLOE, age 9

SOPHIA, age 8

89

WHAT DO YOUR MUM AND DAD SAY ABOUT THE QUEEN?

My Dad says this about the Queen
"The Queen is a great woman and strong,
she being keep the country in a great
and exelent way.

MIA, age 9

My mum says that
the Queen need's to pull her
weight around the cantry
a bit more.

PREYA, age 9

WOULD YOU LIKE TO BE KING OR QUEEN?

I would like to be a king because kings are rich.

RICO, age 9

I woulden't like to be the Queen besause you have to sign alot of papers and it might be boring for me.

KATIE, age 9

I would like to be the queen because I like everthing She dose and I want to live in her house.

JESSIE, age 9

Yes because you have a lemo, enowmas house and people that loves you and people that helps you.

LEAH, age 9

Yes I would like to be King because I like Sighning papers.

OMARI, age 9

MADDIE, age 7

I Wouldnot be a king because you have to be inchrch and you have to chop of peoples heads of?

TAFARI, age 9

93

yes I would because
its very responseable

DOMINIC, age 8

Yes I would like to be Queen
because I would get to travel
the world and help people.

CHLOE, age 9

yes I would
beacouse then
I could boss people
arounnt.

CHRISTOPHER, age 8

CAITLIN, age 7

95

ACKNOWLEDGEMENTS

Michael O'Mara Books would like to thank the following schools for contributing the wonderful, charming and imaginative material in this book: Bourne Westfield Primary Academy; Oasis Academy Shirley Park; Olga Primary School, Tower Hamlets; Pinewood School, Bourton, Wiltshire; and St Bernadette Catholic Junior School, Clapham Park.

We feel sure the queen would appreciate and take delight in each and every one of the entries included.